MW01171186

Of Hope and Purpose

By Dolores Howell

Home Crafted Artistry & Printing
In conjunction with
Miraculous Interventions
Productions

This publication is intended to be poetic representations regarding the subject matters covered. All poems here presented are the author's original work. The poetry, statements and opinions expressed in this book are those of the author. Except for brief quotations and except as permitted under the United States Copyright Act of 1976, no part of this publication may be reproduced or distributed in any form or means without written permission of the publisher, author or assignees.

"Of Hope and Purpose," Copyright 2023 Dolores Howell/Eastern Heights Baptist Church.
Published by Home Crafted Artistry & Printing in conjunction with Miraculous Interventions Productions with permission.

ISBN 13: 9798852686169

Home Crafted Artistry & Printing
2404 Scenic Dr. NE #6
Lanesville, IN 47136

Miraculous Interventions Productions
2045 Kennedy Dr. NW
Corydon, IN 47112

Cover design by Mary Dow Bibb Smith and Deborah Aubrey-Peyron, editors and publishers.
Proudly printed in the United States of America.

Cover art from Clker: camel-silhouette-hi

In memory of my husband,
James Howell,
with gratitude to
Wesley Howell, my grandson
and my many friends and fellow church
members who helped along the way.

Without them, this book would never
have come to be.

Table of Contents

ACKNOWLEDGEMENTS

My husband Jim had a year-long health issue in 2022. My eyes had gotten so bad at the age of 86, the members of my church, friends and family came to my rescue. They drove me to the hospital and rehab center almost daily. They provided me with food for months during this difficult time in my life. Had they not come to my rescue, I simply don't know what I would have done. I thank God for them every day.

Jim passed on October 26th, 2022. I would like to dedicate these poems to my church and close friends who helped me in such hard times. Without you, this would not have been possible.

Chris Gustafson, Minister of Eastern Heights Baptist
Michael Gregg
Ginny Gregg
Steve Hardin
Patt Hardin
Delores (Dee) Cutrera
Kim Karnes
Dora Nevins
Larry Nevins
Lori Fox
Nancy Oberson
Bill Oberson
Jerry Smart
Susan Smart
Jim and Cindy Kanning

Introduction

It was in the early 1980's when Jim called my editor (at the time) about the book I was working on, *"Stand Straight and Grow Tall."*

The editor commented she had to write a poem and she didn't know quite what to write. It was then that Jim brought me into the conversation.

I said, "Poetry is not hard for me to write. You just write your thoughts."

Surprised at my comment-since she knew I couldn't read very well-and was taken aback.

She asked, "What do you know about poetry?"

In response, I quickly wrote a poem for her. She was very surprised at my accumulation of thoughts as I wrote them down. She commented several times, "Your writings are not poetry in the true sense. But I encourage you to keep on writing due to I love the way you write!"

This started me on the road of writing poetry; putting my thoughts down in verse style. And I did it for years.

As life went on, Jim and I happily settled into retirement. My husband took dictation for me for many years. You see, I have always been school-illiterate.

By the year 2022, Jim's health was failing and I had to depend on friends and church members to help me finish my quest.

The members of my church came to my rescue. I thank God for them every day. My friends outside my church also came to my aid. After Jim passed away, I decided I would dedicate this book of poetry to them.

Several went beyond the call of duty as Christians. I did not know how I could ever pull these poems together that I had written over 40-plus years. Since I could not see to read or write them out again, I expressed my concern to Kim, one of the members of my church. She read my writings I had accumulated, and put them together for me.

I also mentioned I could not find an editor as I had been looking for quite a while. I wanted to finish this book so I could finish the second book I was working on.

I had begun to wonder if any of this was going to work, when I received a call from a church member who I barely knew. Her name was Dee.

She said, "I hear you are looking for someone to read your manuscript to you and take dictation."

I replied, "This is true."

Dee went on, "I will read your manuscript and take dictation for you. I will be at your house at 3:30 today."

And she did just that! We worked together on the whole book to lay it out.

Dee and Kim started me on the road to have my book of poetry published.

Then came my grandson Wesley Howell, who made arrangements for editing and publishing.

UNTEACHABLE

When I was a child in school
It was said to my parents who valued education
"Your child is unteachable."

"Unteachable" it was said
By those who are teachable,
By those in the know.

Those in the know marked my records "unteachable."
Many believed "unteachable" was me.
I was in a school for those who were teachable.

I was ignored and ridiculed
Because "unteachable" was me.
I didn't learn much – I was "unteachable."

One day I memorized a poem
A poem for the teachable, and me.
A poem to improve my thinking and myself.

A poem which said what I should be
Even though I was "unteachable."
I took it with me through the years.

Even though I couldn't read and write
Because I was "unteachable."
I have carried the poem in my mind all these years.

I wrote a poem of my own years later,
Even though I couldn't read and write.
It was a good poem, I was told by someone "teachable."

So I wrote another, and another good poem
Good enough to be published,
Said those who are teachable.

"But wait," I said, "that can't be.
"Only the teachable can write poetry
Good enough to be published."

My poem cannot be
Because we all can see I am "unteachable."
Poetry is not for me,
Only the teachable can write poetry.

THE GIFT

When I was a little girl with nothing to do
And feeling lonely,
I sat down on the edge of the porch
With my feet on the cement walk.
It was cloudy and chilly as I sat there
I suddenly felt warmth.
I looked up at the sky to see the sun
Peeking out from behind a dark cloud.
As I sat there enjoying the warmth,
Watching the sunlight,
A thought came into my mind: GOD.

At that moment I knew there was a God.
From that time until this
I have searched for this God.
Sometimes I would find Him;
Sometimes I would not find Him,
No matter how hard I searched.
Sometimes He would feel so close,
And other times so far away.
But He was there, somewhere,
When I really needed Him.
Not when I thought I needed Him.

But when nobody else could help me,
He would be there.
Along this long journey
I somehow learned about Him.
Now, being older,
I look back at the hard times
And the good times.

I have found knowing there is a God
Is the greatest gift I have ever received.

CAN'T YOU HEAR ME?

Is there anybody
To help me through these hard times?
There are people all around me
Who could not see my pain
Even though I tried to tell them.
There were people
Who thought they had everything they needed
To solve any problem.
That was their call.
I called out to God.
Where is my help
That You promised long ago
To ease this burden You gave me?
These people don't hear,
Can't You see?
Surely if they heard me
They would come and help me.
Even though I begged them to listen
They tried,
Then turned their heads away.
My pain is the same as others,
"Can't You see," I told them constantly.
Why God?
Can't You send to me
The help I need to tell those who tried to hear
So I can be free?
"Yes," God said to me.
"I could send you help.
But, you see, the help you really needed
Can only come from Me.
My help will make you free
To see how much you mean to me."

GOD TALKS TO ME

Yes, God talks to me
When my words are unkind.
What does He say?
Does He talk to me
About things that will happen?
Does He talk to me about you -
The things I can see in you
That are disturbing to me.
The things you should do or not do?
No, He does not talk to me about these things.
He talks to me about me,
What I should think and do.
He doesn't talk about you.

JUST BETWEEN YOU AND ME

The day is over, the night is coming.
The sunset that I see and I am as lonely as can be.
As I look at the lovely sunset,
I cry out to You, my God,
That I may feel the warmth of Your love.
Even though I cannot see You or hear Your voice,
Please come to me at night.
Your warm love will be all I need,
When it is just between You and me.
My God, tonight let Your love be just between You and me.
Just between You and me,
I cry out tonight - let Your love be
Just between You and me.

PART TIME GOD

A part time God is not for me.
Are you a listening God and one that doesn't answer?
One that doesn't answer when I pray?
My God, my hope is in You and You
May hear my prayers or not.
My dreams are in You.
But I have learned along life's way
My giving is for You, my service comes from You.
You are my God, my hope
Learning what I need to
Learn from You and get myself through the day.
To others in Your name,
My understanding of others comes from You,
As You have taught me to each day,
As I have learned from You along life's days
I can see my failures come from me,
And not You.
As You can see, a part-time God is not for me.
A God that comes and goes may hear my prayers or not-
You are not a part-time God but there with me
All the day through.

THE HEART OF GOD

What does it take
To touch the heart of God?
I cry out to God:
I know You see my pain.
When will You bring this awful thing to an end?
I have tried so hard.
I know I am not good at being patient
And enduring this awful pain.
But I have tried so hard
As You can see.
I waited, not patiently, but I waited.

I tried to trust in You.
I cried when I knew
That I was not what You thought I should be and do.
I look to You
With my heart in my hand
Asking You to help me, daily
To get through this awful thing
For You to open the doors of Heaven
And let the sun shine in with light
That will give me glorious peace
So I will witness Your glory all around me,
Not for everybody else to see, just me.

Then God answered me:
"Yes, I see your pain,
I also see the good
That came from your pain.
The hope others can see.
Are you trusting me?
I also know
How you waited for Me
And working in you
Every day you grow closer to Me."

18

What does it take
To open the doors of Heaven?

"When the time is right
And you are ready,
I will open the doors of Heaven."

AS LONG AS I HAVE YOU

As I looked across the ocean at the sunset
There was red and yellow across the sky.
The waves were quieter than usual.
I put my guilt, anguish, and heartbreak aside
So I could think about this goodness that God has made.
As I took a deep breath I said slowly to my God,
"When I think of all the things that You have made and
The workings of them that keeps life in motion every day.

I think of the good, oh yes, the bad too, the bad people do,
Over and over although You told us not to.
We learn the hard way we should have listened to You.
We just go on trying not to, thinking of You.
I can't help wondering if You get tired of the bad things
That people do.
Not caring about You.
The bad things that often come from mankind's own
Selfishness
Not from You.
Not caring about the unkind and untrue thoughts we
Have of You.
Or the power in You to end it all with one little thought.
That could be Your call.
Do You get bored and lonely?
Do You long for something else to do that would have
Meaning just for You?"

"Bored?" God answered me.
"Lonely? No," He said.
"I never do nor need I never look for something else to do.
I am God.
I have it all.
Just as long as I have you."

HOPE

Hope.
What we know to be true
Brings you thoughts anew
Thoughts of great and mysterious things
Things of glory that sing of all
You could want to see or hear
That no man has ever seen or heard before.
This hope gives peace and joy
Rings out to all your feelings
Of what you have ever wanted.
God is in this world and all He gives
Is good and peace on earth forevermore.

I WONDER*

When Jesus was a little boy,
Did He walk along the Sea of Galilee and let the water lap
His feet?
I would, wouldn't you?
When Jesus was a little boy,
Did He watch His father plane the wood
And pick up shavings to smell their fragrance?
I would, wouldn't you?
When Jesus was a little boy,
Did He smell the bread baking in the charcoal oven
And ask His mother for a piece?
I would, wouldn't you?
When Jesus was a little boy,
Did He stand on the flat rooftop at night
And look up at sparkling stars?
I would, wouldn't you?
When Jesus was a little boy,
Did He lie on His pallet at night
And thank God for the gifts of the day?
I do, don't you?

*(*editor's favorite)*

MY SOUL LONGS FOR YOU

Jesus, my Lord, I know it is true
That I will someday stand before You.
Then will I know, as I hope every day
Your greatness will wipe all my aching away.
I'll leave tears behind, and hopelessness too
When I am in heaven, looking at You.
Now as I wait, in spite of my fear
I know You've already come to me here.
  Chorus
Jesus, my Lord, my soul longs for You.

DOES GOD HAVE A PLAN FOR ME?

God knows me.
God knows my pain.
Why I cry.
What I want.
What I need.
God knows all about me.
He knows my thoughts before I have them.
He knows my joy before it happens.
He knows my love before I have loved.
He knows all about me.
He knows when to help me.
How to help me.
He knows what to take away from me so I can be free.
He knows all about me.
When pain is so big I can't see
I go to God and say, "Please help me."
I never say, "Do You know what they did to me?"
I have a good God that looks after me.
I cannot see Him, but He saw all of me
Long before I began to be.

THE THREE FACES OF GOD

There are three faces of God.
One face is gentle, kind, warm,
Loving, understanding and compassionate.
Another is strong, firm, insisting and direct
As a teacher should be.
The third is joy, the side that you are,
He is and always will be.
Whether it is a face of being glad
Or a face of insisting or pride,
They are faces that always will be
Concerned with you and me.

WHERE ARE YOU?

Fear makes me feel lonely, tired, and weak.
Why, God, doesn't your strength protect me?
How can I be free?
So many years have passed by me.
Why can't You see I am weary
From the work You gave to me?

Where are you, God?
You seem so far away from me.
Can't You see the hurt in me?
Why don't You know I long for peace?
For victory in what I do?
Why do You let outside friction hurt me,
Scare me?
Why, God, can't You see
I want so much to be free?

WHO KNOWS THE MIND OF GOD?

Who knows the mind of God?
Whoever gave Him anything
To be paid back by Him?
We do know the mind of Christ.

CHRISTMAS

We find that Christmas is coming
Oh, so near.
How much time do we have to get ready?
So much to do.
Gifts to buy with so little money;
I will try to make my loved ones happy
As they think of gifts.
So gladly and generously
It gives such joy to see such happiness in their faces.
Their eyes shine when they sing the song of Christmas.
Of our dear God's Son's birth
So long ago.
Knowing His hand still touches us at Christmas.

When you see your heartbreaking prayers answered
In that moment,
All of your doubtful thoughts are gone.
All of the discouraging words
You have thought and heard for so long
It does not matter.
You just know to let go.
Jesus is Jesus.
He threads the needle and mends all things
Even the heartbreak in me and you.

THIS HAPPENING

In the dark of a sleepless night
I remember the pain of what had happened long ago.
Most who were there had forgotten.
But on this dark night I remembered, and wondered why.
Did I do something wrong?
Could I have stopped it?
Did God punish me for not being good?
Looking carefully, in the quiet darkness of night
I can understand now.
I'm not to blame; it was out of my hands completely.
God did not punish me; He protected me.
Remembering is painful but at last I can rest.
It was someone else's wrong call that led me to
Heartbreaking misery.
I can see, in the darkness of this night, this misery was
Not caused by me.

JESUS, MY GOD, MY ALL

Oh Jesus, my God, my all -
How long will it take?
How long must we wait?
Wait for You?
Oh, Come, come to us.
Jesus, we plead with You.
In all of Your power and glory, we plead with You
To come and save us from our grief.
Jesus, our hope, our joy, come and set us free
As You have done so many times before;
Come, come and save us, from our grief.
Oh God, our Lord, come and save us.

CAN I JUDGE GOD?

Do I have the right to judge God?
After doing all of the things I thought were His desire
The best I knew how.
Walking along the path of pain, grief, heartbreak
And great joy,
Holding tight to the One who led me there
After my best is all finished.
Do I have the right to judge the One
Who knew the path?
Can I look back and see where that path led me
Through the good, sad, happy or bad?
As I look back and see what was given to me
My judgment can only be of His promises
That was there for me.

A part-time God is not for me.
My God my hope is in You.
My dreams are in You.
My giving is for You.
My learning comes from You.
Learning what I need to get
Through life's day.
My understanding of others comes from You
As I learn of You along life's day.
I can see my failures come from me, not You.
So, as you can see a part-time God
Is not for me.
A God that comes and goes
May hear my prayers or not
But there with me all the day through.

FORGIVENESS

Oh my God, my heart is broken
For what I have said and done
That You did not want me to do.
Forgive me, I beg of You.
I am glad I do not need to say forgive me more than a day.
The night will come.
I can rest knowing that You forgave me.

A SONG WE SING

A song we sing
To You, my God, praising Your name.
Song that came from our hearts and our soul.
Our whole body sings from within
The praise of Your name.
We sing like an instrument
That plays the notes that carry through eternity.

HIS KINDNESS IS FOR ALL

Jesus taught us to love one another
With practice and with words.
And His kindness was well served.
Without His example, we would hardly know how to love
Outside of ourselves.
His kindness, all for us.
When Jesus said to God
"Not My will but Your will be done"
This was the kindest thing Jesus has ever done.

DORY'S QUESTION TO GOD

With a broken heart,
With pain and grief
And fear of what is going to be,
I ask my God, "Can't you see my pain, grief and fear?"
He then answered me,
"What kind of house
Would you build for Me?
Brick and mortar on your land so you could see Me?
And what would I do?
I cannot live in this house you would build for Me.
I made the universe.
The earth is just one little part.
And you are like a blade of grass in a large field of grass.
And yet I see your pain, grief and fear.
Knowing that you trust in Me, this too shall pass
Into what you call time.
And you will see My love and goodness is forever
In that time."

QUESTIONING GOD

So you question God?
Is He, as we say?
Does He think of us
In the light that we must obey?
Or!
Is He there, somewhere in a distance far away
That He does not care?
Is He, as we have been told, or is He as we make Him to
be, made of GOLD?
Does He lead us down a path that leaves us cold?
Or does He long for us to seek Him out
So that He can lead us - His way?
But no matter what we want to say,
The good or bad we think,
He is GOD and He will be here to stay
Long after we have gone away.

FOR ME AND MAYBE YOU

I often cried out to God
In the midst of disappointment and heartbreak.
Why do I need to deal with this?
The teachings the scholar said were good for me
And maybe you?
They were not being unkind and cruel
With the things they said to do.
They hoped what they said was right
Without looking too closely to see
If it was really right and true.
It seemed good for me - and maybe you.
But this teaching led to hopelessness and heartbreak
For me - and maybe you.

FROM THE BEGINNING TO THE END

In the womb
We do not have free will.
We will receive what comes to us
In life.
We have the freedom to choose
What we will do.
With all the things that come our way

Bad or good, failure or success.
They come our way or we bring them our way.
We choose what we will do
With the things that come to us:
Our freedom gives us the choice.

But when we come to death's door
The actor may say,
"I made a lot of money...
I played Mother Teresa in a play."
But Mother Teresa, at death's door, will say
"I made a little money, and I put God first."

No matter what we choose in life - good or bad, for God or
Against Him,
We cannot choose in death.
Only God will be the judge
From the beginning to the end.

Come with me and see
All the wonders
Along the path
Waiting for us.
No one else can see
The wonders
Until we show them
The pain we leave behind

Will be but a moment.
The good things we shared
Is what they will cherish.

VICTORY

Now the work is finished
The victory is won.
The victory is here for everyone.
The victory that will always be
For you and me.
The victory of God's caring love -
Victory that now gives us hope through Jesus' victory
That sets us free.
That victory that will last through eternity.

LONG ROAD

Look back behind you
What do you see?
A long road that twists and turns
Through the trees.
What has happened on that road
As you passed through?
Is it fit for someone new?
Whose innocence do you owe much to?
Have you laid markers on the stones
You tripped over?
Like others did before you?

Or did you go on not thinking of someone new
When you traveled that road some others left for you?
Did you leave leaves on the trees and the sky blue?
Or did you leave the trees bare,
Still and lonely, with nothing to do?
Does the creek run free?
Or does it cease to be?
Did you run through, grabbing all, just for you?
Or did you walk through
Taking only what you were due?
Did you travel alone?

ASK

It was a sleepless night for me, as I tossed and turned
When I found myself in a place that gave me concern.
Long lines of people standing before me, as far as I could see.
One at a time was called from the line,
Their names I could hear.

As my turn came near, I could see there were
Only one of two places all of us were going to be.
A man stood there, his speech was kind,
Holding a big book, big enough to hold all of time.

"Come," he said to the man before me
"Come and see what is going to be."
The man took his hand and never said a word as he
Walked toward a light that almost blinded me.
Only his face showed his glee
Peaceful, joyful as can be.

A sigh came from the woman behind me,
"It is He."
"Who?" I asked anxiously.
"The one I have longed all my life to see."

Before I could say anymore, He motioned to me.
A man, a man as perfect as can be.
Strong as a God, as He looked at me.
He was the one I too had longed all my life to see.
Perfect, perfect as can be.

As His loving eyes looked at me,
I knew He didn't recognize me.
My whole life was suddenly before me.
His eyes became sad as He looked at me.
Why didn't He hold his hands out to me?
As He had so many times when I could see my life before me?

He asked my name quietly.
I hesitated and spoke it shamefully;
He looked at the big book,
Then looked back at me.

A chill came over me.
"Look at my life," I said to him.
"It is good, better than the man before me.
He helped you so generously, through the pains that were
just as great in me.
You never helped me, and now You can't see my name.
How can this be, if You are just, true and kind?
Why didn't You come to me?"

His eyes became sadder as He said to me,
"It was My want, to come to you
To help you through the pains.
To give you all the life I had to give
So you would know Me, just, true and kind.
But, you see, you never asked Me."

JUST FOR A LITTLE

Walking along the beach in the fog, peacefully,
Thinking of what the day would bring.
Golf, I thought, a good round of golf
Will make the day joyful.
But how can this be? The fog is getting thicker.
Oh my! Golf may not be this day.
So my most favorite thing may not be.
I lifted my hands to the sky
And shouted so loudly,
"Oh God! Where is the sun?"

Then God answered me.
"The fog is the problem.
When it lifts you will see
The sun will be there
ALWAYS
Right where it will remain."

To accept You my God, as You are;
Not as I want You to be.
Powerful enough-
That I would be brought through life
Perfect and unscathed, because I am SAVED.

Now, as I see through grace
The scathing is what brought You closer to me.
As I was being prepared for eternity.
Eternity, I long to see
That is there with You, for me.

In One Moment

I look for the moment Jesus will come to me.
Come to me, Oh come to me.
Jesus, come to me is my plea.
My heart is full of sadness
From this misunderstood thing
That has come to me.
My strength is almost joy.
I try to hold on.
Oh, Jesus, come to me.
As I wait for You to come home and set me free.

Also by this author:

Stand Straight and Grow Tall

is Dory's true story of her lifetime struggle against illiteracy. Dory's story is the story, of so many in our society even today, and they are not just school children. Dory tells of her struggle with words, and with educators, administrators, counselors, psychologists – even with God. How could God let her go through all of this? Yet it is her faith in God that kept her going.

Dory's story is one of hope and holds valuable lessons for all who come in contact with people with learning disabilities, not just parents and educators. Understanding how dyslexia effects a person's perceptions and the problems this disability causes, is the first step to understanding how to educate dyslexic persons.

This revised edition of "Stand Straight and Grow Tall" has updated content and contains some of Dolores' poetry and prose, not in the original edition. Published by Home Crafted Artistry & Printing.

Available from Amazon.com

See this and other fine books at: HomeCraftedArtistry.com

Made in the USA
Columbia, SC
26 April 2024

34672794R00029